A STEP TO YOUR DESTINATION:

HOW TO ADD ZEROS TO YOUR INCOME EVERYDAY

BY

MATTHEW RICHES

Dedication

To the visionaries, innovators, and
relentless pursuers of possibility,
whose audacious dreams have reshaped
industries, inspired generations, and
propelled humanity forward.
Bill Gates, whose pioneering spirit and
commitment to technology have
revolutionized the way we live, work, and
connect with the world.
To Elon Musk, whose boundless
imagination and unwavering determination
have propelled us toward the frontiers of
space exploration, sustainable energy, and
transportation innovation.
To all the genius entrepreneurs who dare to
challenge the status quo, defy the odds, and
envision a future defined by ingenuity,
resilience, and limitless potential.
This book is dedicated to you—the
architects of tomorrow, the catalysts of
change, and the trailblazers of innovation—
who remind us that every step toward our
destination is an opportunity to redefine

what is possible and shape the world we aspire to create.

Your visionary leadership, unwavering courage, and relentless pursuit of excellence serve as beacons of inspiration for us all.

May your brilliance continue to illuminate the path forward, guiding us toward a future filled with boundless opportunities, transformative breakthroughs, and enduring impact.

With profound gratitude and admiration,

[MATTHEW RICHES]

TABLE OF CONTENTS

INTRODUCTION

Individuals, groups, and nations have been driven throughout human history to investigate various routes that can lead to financial success and prosperity. The desire for money has been an eternal aspiration as well. A significant factor in determining the economic landscape and the well-being of societies is wealth, which is typically assessed in terms of financial assets, properties, and resources. Wealth plays a crucial role in shaping the economic landscape. Entrepreneurial initiatives, strategic investments, innovative ideas, and responsible financial management are all components of the journey toward wealth development, which is characterized by a complex interaction of economic, social, and individual elements. During this investigation of the process by which wealth is produced, we delve into the myriad of factors that contribute to the development and accumulation of wealth. We also investigate the dynamics that move individuals and nations toward economic success and sustained financial growth. In the quest for prosperity, there are a variety of ways to generate money, ranging from business initiatives to investment techniques. This diversity is a reflection of the dynamic and ever-changing nature of economies.

CHAPTER 1
Things to Do to Generate Income from Business

To produce cash from company ideas, one must possess creative thinking, problem-solving skills, and a grasp of the requirements of the market. The following are many methods that can assist you in discovering profitable business ideas:

1. Identify Your Interests and Talents: Think about the things that you are enthusiastic about and the talents that you have. Chances in a company that is a good fit for your skills and interests can be found by following your interests and looking for chances.

2. It is important to be abreast of the latest market trends, including those about developing technology, changing customer tastes, and industry trends. Keep an eye out for voids in or any places where the

solutions that are the market already available can be enhanced.

3. **Solve difficulties:** identify prevalent difficulties or pain areas that people confront in their daily lives or within specialized sectors. Develop solutions that solve these concerns effectively.

4. **Research Target Audiences:** Understand the needs, preferences, and behaviors of your target audience. Conduct surveys, interviews, and market research to acquire insights into consumer desires and preferences.

5. **Explore Niche Markets:** Consider niche markets or underdeveloped demographics that have specific requirements or interests. Catering to specific markets can help you stand out and establish a loyal consumer base.

6. **Utilize Your Network:** Reach out to friends, family, coworkers, and industry contacts for brainstorming sessions or comments on new company ideas.

Networking can also help you identify chances and connect with possible partners or mentors.

7. **Follow Your Passions:** Pursue business ideas that correspond with your interests and principles. Building a business around something you are passionate about might enhance your drive and fulfillment.

8. **Evaluate Competitors:** Analyze existing businesses within your sector or niche to determine their strengths, flaws, and areas for improvement. Look for ways to differentiate your goods and bring distinct value to customers.

9. **Consider Online Trends:** Explore online trends, such as e-commerce, digital services, remote work solutions, and online education. The Internet offers several chances for beginning and developing enterprises with few overhead costs.

10. **Experiment and iterate:** Don't be hesitant to experiment with different company ideas and approaches. Start small,

test your concepts, gain feedback, and iterate based on the outcomes. Failure is frequently a wonderful learning experience on the route to success.

11. **Evaluate Profitability:** Assess the income potential, scalability, and profitability of each company idea. Consider aspects such as start-up expenses, profit margins, market demand, and growth potential.

12. **Seek Inspiration Everywhere:** Inspiration can come from different sources, including books, podcasts, industry events, and everyday encounters. Stay interested and open-minded to new ideas and chances. By combining these tactics and keeping proactive in your hunt for business ideas, you can boost your chances of finding attractive opportunities to create revenue. Remember that entrepreneurship needs dedication, tenacity, and a willingness to adapt to changing market conditions.

How to Determine Your Interests and Skills for Earning Income

Identifying your interests and skills to make cash entails introspection, self-assessment, and exploring options that correspond with your passions and strengths. Here's how you can go about it:

1. **"Ponder on Your Passions"**: Take some time to ponder the activities, interests, and topics that fascinate you. What do you enjoy doing in your free time? What themes or subjects do you find yourself drawn to? Your passions can provide vital information regarding prospective income-generating options.

2. **Assess your abilities and strengths:** Make a list of your abilities, talents, and strengths. These can include both hard talents (such as programming, writing, and graphic design) and soft skills (such as communication, problem-solving, and

leadership). Consider experiences from your education, career, hobbies, and personal life.

3. **Identify transferable skills:** identify skills that can be applied across other industries or work roles. For example, if you have good communication abilities, you could seek jobs in writing, public speaking, marketing, or customer service.

4. **Consider Past Experiences:** Reflect on past experiences, including jobs, internships, volunteer work, and educational projects. What jobs or responsibilities did you like the most? What accomplishments are you proud of? Analyze the components of these encounters that you felt were fulfilling or rewarding.

5. **Seek input:** Reach out to friends, family members, mentors, and colleagues for input on your abilities and strengths. Sometimes, others may identify abilities or qualities in you that you might overlook.

6. **Explore new activities and opportunities:** Be open to attempting new

activities, hobbies, or experiences that pique your interest. Attend courses, classes, or events relevant to the issues you're curious about. Exploring new hobbies might help you find hidden talents and interests.

7. **Assess Market Demand:** Evaluate the demand and possible profitability of diverse talents and interests in the labor market or business landscape. Research industries, sectors, and employment roles that are experiencing growth and a need for specific talents.

8. **Combine hobbies and abilities:** Look for chances to combine your hobbies and abilities to generate unique value propositions. For example, if you have a passion for photography and great editing skills, you could investigate freelance photography or create an internet photography business.

9. **Seek Inspiration:** Seek inspiration from successful people who have created jobs or enterprises around their passions and

strengths. Read biographies, listen to interviews, and examine case studies of people who have turned their interests into successful companies.

10. **Stay Flexible and Open-Minded:** Keep in mind that your hobbies and skills may vary over time. Stay flexible and open-minded as you explore new options and professional trajectories. Be willing to change and pivot based on shifting interests, market trends, and possibilities.

By taking a proactive approach to identifying your interests and skills, you can unearth prospective income-generating opportunities that connect with your passions and strengths. Remember that finding the correct fit may require time, experimentation, and a willingness to explore new possibilities.

HOW TO OBSERVE MARKET TRENDS

Believing in observing market trends is vital for individuals and companies striving for success in today's dynamic business environment. Here's why cultivating belief in observing market patterns is crucial:

1. **Insight into Consumer Behavior:** Market trends offer useful insights into consumer behavior, tastes, and purchase patterns. By analyzing trends, businesses may discover what motivates their target audience and modify their products or services accordingly.

2. **Identifying Growth Possibilities:** Monitoring market trends helps firms uncover new growth possibilities and emerging markets. Whether it's discovering undiscovered niches or capitalizing on evolving customer wants, staying alert to trends enables firms to increase their market

reach.

3. **Strategic Decision-Making:** Informed decision-making relies on a complete understanding of market dynamics. By studying trends, firms can make strategic decisions regarding product development, marketing strategies, pricing, and resource allocation, therefore maximizing their chances of success.

4. **Competitive Advantage:** Keeping abreast of market trends provides a competitive edge by helping organizations predict and respond to developments faster than their competitors. By staying ahead of the curve, firms can position themselves as industry leaders and achieve a competitive edge.

5. **Risk Management:** Market trends can act as early indicators of potential risks and dangers to firms. By anticipating shifts in consumer preferences, economic conditions, or regulatory environments, firms can

proactively reduce risks and adapt their plans to limit negative repercussions.

6. **Innovation and Adaptability:** Market developments often generate innovation and drive organizational change. By adopting trends, organizations can reinvent products, services, and business models to better satisfy shifting customer wants and stay relevant in a fast-changing market environment.

7. **Enhanced Customer Engagement:** Understanding market trends enables firms to engage with customers more effectively. By connecting their offers with emerging issues, interests, and worries, firms may establish deeper connections with their audience and build brand loyalty over time.

8. **Future Planning and Forecasting:** Observing market patterns provides useful information for long-term planning and forecasting. By studying past data and monitoring developing trends, firms can forecast future developments and establish

strategic initiatives to capitalize on upcoming opportunities.

9. Adapting to Technological Advances: Technological developments typically generate shifts in consumer behavior and market dynamics. By observing trends in technology adoption and innovation, businesses may harness new tools and platforms to improve operations, enhance customer experiences, and gain a competitive edge.

10. Continuous Learning and Improvement: Believing in tracking market trends develops a culture of continuous learning and improvement within firms. By encouraging staff to stay aware, interested, and proactive about market trends, firms may stimulate innovation, creativity, and adaptation at all levels.

In conclusion, embracing the idea of observing market trends is crucial for organizations to grow, develop, and maintain a competitive advantage in today's fast-paced and ever-changing business scene. By recognizing the necessity of staying aware, adaptive, and sensitive to market dynamics, companies can position themselves for long-term success and sustainable growth.

HOW TO EARN INCOME BY SOLVING PROBLEMS

Believing in the ability to solve issues is crucial for personal growth, professional achievement, and societal progress. Here's why nurturing a belief in problem-solving is crucial, along with some examples:

1. **Empowerment:** Believing in problem-solving empowers individuals to take control of their situations and conquer problems. It instills confidence in one's abilities to handle difficulties and create successful solutions.
Example: A student encountering difficulty understanding complicated mathematical

concepts believes in their problem-solving skills and seeks out additional resources, such as tutoring or online courses, to master the subject.

2. **Innovation:** Problem-solving promotes innovation by enabling individuals to think creatively and explore new ideas. It inspires the development of imaginative ideas to address current challenges and improve existing procedures.

Example: An entrepreneur recognizes a gap in the market for eco-friendly packaging solutions and produces a biodegradable alternative using sustainable materials, displaying a commitment to tackling environmental concerns.

3. **Resilience:** Belief in problem-solving builds resilience in the face of adversity. It encourages individuals to persevere despite setbacks, learn from failures, and adjust their ways until they reach desired objectives.

Example: A small business owner confronts financial difficulties during an economic downturn but remains resilient by investigating cost-cutting methods, diversifying revenue streams, and getting aid from financial advisers to overcome the issues.

4. **Continuous Improvement:** Embracing problem-solving encourages a culture of continuous improvement within organizations and communities. It motivates individuals to seek criticism, identify areas for growth, and execute measures to boost performance and effectiveness.

Example: A nonprofit organization devoted to tackling homelessness performs regular reviews of its programs and services, asking for input from stakeholders and implementing evidence-based interventions to better meet the needs of the community.

5. **Collaboration:** Problem-solving frequently entails collaboration and teamwork, as individuals offer varied viewpoints, expertise, and resources to solve complicated situations collectively. It

generates synergy and encourages cooperation towards common goals.

Example: A cross-functional team within a technology company collaborates to troubleshoot a software bug, calling on the knowledge of software engineers, quality assurance specialists, and customer service personnel to diagnose and resolve the issue immediately.

6. **Impactful Change:** Belief in problem-solving generates meaningful change and societal impact by tackling structural concerns, fighting for equity and justice, and pushing constructive transformation in society.

Example: Social activists mobilize communities to address racial inequity by organizing nonviolent protests, pushing for policy reforms, and fostering conversation to increase understanding and unity among varied groups.

7. **Personal Fulfillment:** Successfully overcoming difficulties offers a sense of

success and fulfillment, reaffirming one's belief in their talents and driving further growth and development.

Example: A volunteer dedicates time and resources to help humanitarian efforts in disaster-stricken countries, offering crucial aid and assistance to afflicted communities and finding tremendous personal satisfaction from making a good difference in the lives of others.

In summary, creating a belief in problem-solving is crucial for individuals and organizations to negotiate problems, generate creativity, build resilience, and influence positive change in the world. By embracing a problem-solving mindset, individuals may overcome difficulties, seize opportunities, and realize their maximum potential, both personally and professionally.

CHAPTER 2
MIND-CHANGING CONCEPT OF GENERATING MONEY

The mind-changing notion of acquiring wealth entails modifying one's mindset and beliefs regarding wealth accumulation, financial success, and abundance. It comprises adopting a constructive and proactive approach towards creating wealth, seizing opportunities, and managing resources effectively. Here are the major parts of this concept:

1. **Abundance mindset:** Embracing an abundance mindset is crucial to the concept of gaining riches. Instead of considering wealth as finite and scarce, those with an abundance mindset feel that possibilities for financial success are abundant and available to all. They focus on possibilities, abundance, and producing value rather than obsessing over restrictions and poverty.

2. **Focus on Value Creation:** Earning riches frequently entails focusing on producing value for others. Rather than just seeking financial gain, individuals and businesses prioritize offering products, services, or solutions that address actual needs and bring substantial benefits to customers or clients. By focusing on value creation, wealth naturally follows as a by-product of offering value to others.

3. **Entrepreneurial mindset:** Adopting an entrepreneurial mindset requires embracing risk-taking, innovation, and a willingness to pursue opportunities outside of normal channels. Entrepreneurs know that developing wealth frequently entails stepping into unfamiliar areas, seizing chances, and embracing failure as a learning experience on the route to success.

4. **Financial Literacy and Education:** Earning money requires a solid foundation of financial literacy and education. Individuals must understand basic financial

principles, such as budgeting, saving, investing, and managing debt, to make informed decisions about their money. Continuous learning and self-education play essential roles in acquiring financial concepts and methods.

5. **Goal Setting and Planning:** Setting clear financial objectives and implementing concrete plans are critical components of gaining money. Individuals who aim to develop money identify their objectives, establish deadlines, and break down their ambitions into doable steps. They periodically examine and change their plans as they go towards achieving their financial aspirations.

6. **Building Multiple Income Streams:** Diversifying income streams is a crucial approach for earning wealth and limiting risk. Rather than relying entirely on a single source of income, individuals explore opportunities to produce income from several sources, such as investments,

entrepreneurship, freelance work, passive income streams, and side hustles. Diversification promotes financial stability and resilience.

7. **Mindset of Continuous Progress:**
Earning riches is not just about amassing money but also about personal and professional progress. Individuals committed to achieving riches embrace a mindset of constant learning, self-improvement, and growth. They invest in strengthening their abilities, expanding their knowledge, and building positive habits that contribute to their success over the long run.

8. **Generosity and Giving Back:**
Cultivating a spirit of generosity and giving back to others is a fundamental component of the concept of achieving riches. Individuals who have achieved financial success frequently feel joy in using their wealth to have a positive effect in their communities, support philanthropic causes, and contribute to the well-being of others.

In summary, the mind-changing concept of earning wealth involves embracing an abundance mindset, focusing on value creation, adopting an entrepreneurial mindset, prioritizing financial literacy and education, setting clear goals and plans, diversifying income streams, embracing continuous growth, and cultivating a spirit of generosity. By adjusting one's mindset and ideas about wealth, individuals can unlock their full ability to acquire wealth and create a life of abundance and fulfillment.

How does negative thinking affect getting rich?

Negative thinking can considerably impair the process of getting rich and achieving financial success in various ways.
1. **Limiting Beliefs:** Negative thinking typically leads to limiting beliefs about one's ability and prospects for achievement. If

individuals believe that they are not capable of attaining money or that financial success is reserved for others, they may not actively pursue opportunities or take the necessary risks to enhance their wealth.

2. **Fear of Failure:** Negative thinking promotes fear of failure, which can freeze individuals from taking action towards their financial goals. Fear of failure may deter individuals from embracing chances, starting enterprises, or investing in ventures that have the potential to generate riches.

3. **Lack of Confidence:** Negative thinking impairs confidence and self-esteem, making it harder for individuals to assert themselves, bargain successfully, or take measured risks in pursuit of wealth-building opportunities. Without confidence in their talents, individuals may shy away from challenges or settle for mediocrity instead of striving for perfection.

4. **Focus on hurdles:** Negative thinking tends to accentuate hurdles and challenges

rather than concentrate on alternatives and solutions. Instead of perceiving setbacks as temporary challenges to overcome, individuals may become overwhelmed by difficulties and failures, leading to procrastination or giving up on their financial goals altogether.

5. **Self-Sabotage:** Negative thinking can appear as self-sabotaging behaviors that impair progress towards wealth-building objectives. Individuals may indulge in detrimental habits such as overspending, procrastination, or impulsivity, which can derail financial ambitions and impair long-term success.

6. **Limited Risk-Taking:** Negative thinking typically develops a risk-averse mindset, where individuals are reluctant to venture outside their comfort zones or explore chances that involve uncertainty. Without taking reasonable risks, individuals may miss out on potential routes for wealth generation and growth.

7. **Attracting Negativity:** Negative thinking can attract more negativity into one's life, producing a cycle of pessimism and stagnation. Negative attitudes may repel chances, positive relationships, and favorable conditions that could contribute to financial success.

8. **Inhibiting Innovation and Creativity:** Negative thinking stifles innovation and creativity by deterring individuals from exploring new ideas, trying unique ways, or challenging the status quo. Without a mindset that encourages innovation, individuals may struggle to develop new solutions or capitalize on emerging trends in their quest for riches.

In summary, negative thinking can have profound consequences on the journey towards getting rich by limiting beliefs, fostering fear of failure, undermining confidence, focusing on obstacles, promoting self-sabotage, inhibiting risk-taking, attracting negativity, and inhibiting innovation and creativity. To overcome negative thinking and unlock their potential for financial success, individuals must establish a positive mindset, develop resilience in the face of obstacles, and embrace proactive ways to pursue their wealth-building goals with dedication and optimism.

How is it important to have positive energy toward wealth-making?

Having good energy toward wealth-making is crucial for various reasons:

1. **Mindset Matters:** Positive energy influences mindset. When you approach wealth-making with enthusiasm, you're more likely to have a growth mindset, which encourages resilience, adaptability, and a readiness to learn from challenges and disappointments.

2. **Attracts Opportunities:** Positive energy

tends to attract opportunities. When you radiate happiness, you're more likely to identify and seize opportunities for money creation that may have otherwise gone unnoticed. People are drawn to individuals with positive energy, which can lead to advantageous collaborations, partnerships, and networking opportunities.

3. **Improves Confidence:** Positive energy improves confidence and self-belief. Believing in your abilities to achieve financial success is half the battle. When you approach wealth-making with positivity, you're more likely to make daring decisions, express yourself in negotiations, and pursue ambitious goals with dedication and passion.

4. **Boosts problem-solving skills:** Positive energy boosts problem-solving skills. When faced with challenges or failures, those with a positive mindset are more likely to tackle problems with optimism, inventiveness, and a solutions-oriented mindset. This enables them to overcome obstacles more effectively

and discover inventive solutions to challenging challenges.

5. **Builds Resilience:** Positive energy builds resilience in the face of hardship. Building wealth needs effort and tenacity, as setbacks and failures are inevitable along the way. Maintaining a positive mindset helps individuals bounce back from losses, learn from failures, and stay focused on their long-term goals despite short setbacks.

6. **Improves Well-Being:** Positive energy adds to general well-being and life satisfaction. When you approach wealth-making with a positive mindset, you're more likely to enjoy greater levels of happiness, contentment, and satisfaction in your life. This positive approach can have rippling effects throughout different areas of your life, including relationships, health, and personal fulfillment.

7. **Inspires Others:** Positive energy is contagious and inspires others. When you radiate optimism in your pursuit of wealth-

making, you become a source of inspiration and motivation for everyone around you. Your energy, optimism, and resilience can boost others and create a supportive environment favorable to collaborative success.

8. **Cultivates Gratitude:** Positive energy cultivates gratitude and appreciation for what you have achieved and the chances accessible to you. Gratitude is a strong mindset that creates contentment, abundance, and a sense of fulfillment in life. By practicing thankfulness during your wealth-making journey, you may keep perspective, stay grounded, and recognize the gifts in your life.

In summary, having positive energy toward wealth-making is crucial because it changes mindsets, attracts opportunities, builds confidence, enhances problem-solving skills, fosters resilience, improves well-being, inspires others, and cultivates thankfulness. By embracing positivism in your quest for financial success, you can unlock your full potential, overcome challenges, and create a life of wealth and fulfillment.

HOW CONSISTENCY ACCELERATES INCOME IN SKILLS DEVELOPMENT

Consistency in increasing abilities can enhance income development in numerous ways.

1. **Continuous Growth:** Consistently working on developing your skills ensures that you are continually becoming better at what you do. Over time, this progress leads to increased expertise, efficiency, and effectiveness in your profession, which can translate into higher earning potential.

2. **Value proposition:** As you increase your talents, you raise the value you can offer employers, clients, or customers. Consistently delivering high-quality work

and exhibiting competence in your sector makes you more popular and valuable in the marketplace, allowing you to command better rates or wages.

3. **Competitive Advantage:** Consistency in skill progress offers you a competitive advantage over others in your field. By remaining current on the newest trends, technologies, and best practices, you position yourself as a top performer capable of delivering extraordinary results, which can open doors to better-paying opportunities and professional development.

4. **Building Reputation:** Consistently developing your talents helps build a positive reputation within your industry or expertise. When you regularly deliver high-quality work and exhibit a commitment to excellence, you acquire the trust and respect of colleagues, clients, and employers, which can lead to referrals, recommendations, and new revenue prospects.

5. **Adaptability:** Consistently developing

your skills makes you more adaptable to changes in the job market and industry trends. As technology progresses and new challenges emerge, people with a habit of continual learning and skill development are better positioned to handle change, grasp opportunities, and stay relevant, eventually increasing income growth.

6. **Networking chances:** Consistency in skill growth typically leads to networking chances with other professionals in your sector. Engaging with colleagues, attending industry events, and participating in professional development activities can expose you to fresh ideas, collaborations, and prospective income-generating relationships.

7. **Positioning for Promotions and Hikes:** In many circumstances, persistent skill growth can lead to promotions, salary hikes, and advancement opportunities within your existing organization. Employers reward employees who display a commitment to

personal and professional progress and are more likely to invest in those who show potential for additional responsibilities and contributions.

8. **Diversification of revenue streams:** Consistently upgrading your talents opens up opportunities to diversify your revenue streams. By improving your skill set and researching new areas of knowledge, you can seek freelance work, consulting opportunities, side projects, or entrepreneurial initiatives that can supplement your primary income and accelerate overall income growth.

In short, constancy in increasing your abilities is a major driver of income increases. By committing to continual learning, development, and refinement of your abilities, you position yourself for greater success, improved earning potential, and long-term financial security in your chosen industry or sector.

How does procrastination affect getting rich?

Procrastination can have harmful impacts on the route toward getting rich in numerous ways.

1. **Delayed Action:** Procrastination typically leads to delayed action on crucial tasks and goals connected to wealth-building. Individuals who delay may postpone making efforts to enhance their income, invest prudently, or seek entrepreneurial opportunities, therefore missing out on potential wealth accumulation over time.

2. **Missed Opportunities:** Procrastination might result in missed opportunities for financial growth and progress. Opportunities for job progression, investment, or entrepreneurship may have a limited window of availability, and postponing action might result in missing out on ideal circumstances for wealth generation.

3. **Compounded Impact of Time:** Time is a significant aspect of wealth accumulation due to the compounding effect of investments and income-generating activities. Procrastination robs individuals of important time that may be used to invest, save, and develop money. The longer one procrastinates, the greater the opportunity cost in terms of lost potential revenues and returns on investments.

4. **Greater Stress and Anxiety:** Procrastination typically leads to greater stress and anxiety as deadlines approach and tasks stack. The strain of imminent deadlines and neglected financial responsibilities can produce a sense of overwhelm and inhibit productivity, further compounding financial issues and impeding progress toward wealth-building goals.

5. **Lack of Financial Discipline:** Procrastination can contribute to a lack of financial discipline and impulse spending tendencies. Individuals who procrastinate

may delay budgeting, savings, and investment planning, resulting in a cycle of financial instability, debt buildup, and missed opportunities for wealth growth.

6. **Loss of Momentum:** Procrastination destroys momentum and consistency in pursuing wealth-building activities. Success in money growth frequently takes persistent effort, discipline, and attention over time. Procrastination interrupts this momentum, making it harder to achieve substantial progress toward financial goals.

7. **Negative Impact on Reputation and Relationships:** Chronic procrastination can negatively impact one's reputation and relationships in professional and personal circumstances. Procrastination may lead to missed deadlines, broken commitments, and strained relationships with employers, clients, or business partners, limiting possibilities for career advancement and financial success.

8. **Inertia and Complacency:**

Procrastination can generate a sense of inertia and complacency, making it tough to move out of comfort zones and pursue new chances for wealth creation. Individuals may get resigned to their current financial conditions and fail to take proactive actions to improve their financial situation, creating a cycle of stagnation and mediocrity.

Procrastination can significantly hinder the journey toward getting rich by delaying action, causing missed opportunities, increasing stress and anxiety, undermining financial discipline, disrupting momentum, damaging relationships, fostering complacency, and perpetuating a cycle of inertia. Overcoming procrastination and taking persistent, proactive measures toward wealth-building goals is vital for achieving financial success and fulfilling one's full potential.

CHAPTER 3
MAKE MONEY WHILE SLEEPING

The concept of creating wealth while sleeping refers to passive income, which is income that is created with minimal effort or ongoing involvement once the initial investment of time, money, or resources has been made. Passive income streams continue to create revenue even when individuals are not actively working or trading their time for money. Here are various methods by which people can create wealth while sleeping. Investing in Stocks and Bonds: Investing in stocks, bonds, mutual funds, and other financial instruments can create passive income through dividends, interest payments, and capital appreciation. By purchasing assets that develop in value over time or provide regular distributions, investors can earn passive income without actively managing their investments on a day-to-day basis.

Beliefs about investing in stocks and bonds differ among individuals and are impacted by factors such as risk tolerance, financial goals, market conditions, and personal beliefs. Here are some typical views and perspectives about investing in stocks and bonds:

1. **Long-Term Growth Potential:** Many investors believe that investing in stocks and bonds offers long-term growth potential for their investment portfolios. Historically, both stocks and bonds have generated returns that outperform inflation over the long run, allowing investors to grow wealth and meet financial goals such as retirement or wealth preservation.

2. **Diversification:** Belief in diversification is a key principle of investing in stocks and bonds. Diversifying across different asset classes, sectors, industries, and geographic

locations can help manage risk and reduce the impact of market volatility on investment portfolios. Many investors believe that diversification is vital for establishing durable and balanced investment portfolios.

3. **Income Generation:** Bonds are frequently seen as income-generating instruments that offer monthly interest payments to bondholders. Investors who prioritize income generation and capital preservation may assume that investing in bonds can provide a continuous source of income, particularly in low-interest-rate settings or during periods of market volatility.

4. **Risk vs. Reward:** Belief about investing in stocks and bonds frequently revolves around the concept of risk versus reward. Stocks are often considered to be riskier investments than bonds, as they are prone to more price volatility and market swings. However, equities also have the potential to

generate larger returns over the long term compared to bonds. Investors may analyze their risk tolerance and investing objectives to find the optimal mix between stocks and bonds in their portfolios.

5. **Market Timing:** Some investors believe in the importance of market timing, attempting to buy stocks and bonds when prices are thought to be low and sell when prices are high. However, market timing can be difficult to execute successfully, and many investors believe in the virtues of a disciplined, long-term investment approach that focuses on asset allocation, diversification, and periodic portfolio rebalancing.

6. **Value Investing vs. Growth Investing:** Belief in distinct investment styles, such as value investing and growth investing, can impact investors' decisions about investing in stocks and bonds. Value investors seek undervalued stocks trading below their real value, whereas growth investors focus on

companies with great growth potential and expectations for future earnings growth. Investors may adopt different investing strategies based on their ideas about market inefficiencies and investment possibilities.

7. **Environmental, Social, and Governance (ESG) Investing:**

Increasingly, investors are considering environmental, social, and governance (ESG) concerns in their investment decisions. Belief in ESG investing indicates a growing awareness of sustainability, corporate responsibility, and ethical issues among investors, who strive to align their investment portfolios with their values and convictions about social and environmental stewardship.

In summary, beliefs about investing in stocks and bonds are impacted by individual preferences, investment objectives, risk tolerance, and market forecasts. While some investors prioritize long-term growth potential and income production, others focus on risk management, diversification, and alignment with personal values. Ultimately, the decision to invest in stocks and bonds should be based on a thorough analysis of individual circumstances, financial goals, and investment philosophy.

OTHER SOURCE OF INCOME GENERATION

Real Estate Investments: Real estate investments, such as rental properties, can create passive income through rental payments from tenants. Real estate investors can purchase properties, lease them to tenants, and receive rental money regularly, delivering a constant stream of passive income while sleeping.

Beliefs about real estate investing vary greatly across individuals and are impacted by factors such as personal experiences, financial aspirations, risk tolerance, market conditions, and cultural attitudes. Here are some prevalent attitudes and perspectives about real estate investment:

1. **Tangible Asset:** Many investors believe that real estate investment has the advantage of owning a tangible asset with inherent worth. Unlike stocks or bonds, which reflect ownership or debt in a firm, real estate investments offer investors actual properties such as land, residential residences, commercial buildings, or rental units that can be utilized, rented, or sold for profit.

2. **Appreciation Potential:** One of the key concepts about real estate investing is its potential for long-term appreciation in value. Historically, real estate values have tended to improve over time, offering investors the chance to acquire wealth and equity through property appreciation. Investors may feel that real estate can serve as a hedge against inflation and a store of value over the long run.

3. **Income Generation:** Real estate investing is often considered a source of

passive income through rental payments from tenants. Investors who purchase rental properties or income-producing real estate assets think that rental income can provide a consistent stream of cash flow and act as a source of passive income, supplementing other sources of income and supporting financial goals such as retirement or wealth creation.

4. **Diversification:** Belief in diversification is also a widespread perspective among real estate investors. Diversifying your portfolios across several asset classes, including stocks, bonds, and real estate, can help manage risk and reduce the impact of market volatility on investment returns. Real estate investments may offer diversification benefits by providing exposure to alternative assets with a possibly low correlation to traditional financial markets.

5. **Leverage:** Real estate investors generally believe in the advantages of leverage, or using borrowed funds to finance property

acquisitions. By leveraging debt financing, investors can amplify returns on investment and boost their purchasing power, allowing them to acquire properties with relatively small amounts of original capital. However, leveraging also increases investment risk and financial vulnerability, as investors are obligated to repay borrowed cash regardless of property performance.

6. **Tax Benefits:** Real estate investment offers numerous tax advantages and incentives that can help investors avoid tax costs and maximize after-tax returns. Beliefs about real estate tax benefits may include deductions for mortgage interest, property taxes, depreciation, and capital gains deferment through like-kind exchanges or 1031 exchanges.

7. **Hands-on Management:** Real estate ownership often requires direct involvement in property management, maintenance, tenant relations, and regulatory compliance. Some investors believe in the benefits of

hands-on management and direct control over their real estate holdings, while others choose to assign management tasks to third-party property managers or real estate specialists.

8. **Market Timing and Location:** Belief in the relevance of market timing and location selection is another crucial element for real estate investors. Investors may believe in identifying inexpensive or emerging economies with great growth potential and positive economic fundamentals. Location-specific considerations such as accessibility to amenities, schools, transit, job areas, and demographic trends can strongly influence real estate investment decisions and outcomes.

In summary, attitudes regarding real estate investment are impacted by individual preferences, investment objectives, risk tolerance, and market forecasts. While some investors target long-term appreciation, income creation, and tax advantages, others focus on leveraging, diversification, and hands-on management. Ultimately, the decision to invest in real estate should be founded on a thorough analysis of individual circumstances, financial goals, and investment philosophy.

Dividend-paying assets: Dividend-paying assets, such as dividend stocks, real estate investment trusts (REITs), and dividend-paying mutual funds, can provide a source of passive income through regular dividend payments to investors. By investing in companies that distribute a percentage of their revenues to shareholders, investors can receive passive income without actively engaging in the operations of the business.

Royalties and Licensing Fees: Individuals who generate intellectual property, such as books, music, software, or patents, can receive passive income through royalties and licensing fees. By licensing their creations to third parties or collecting royalties on sales, creators can create recurring money from their intellectual property while sleeping.

Peer-to-Peer Lending: Peer-to-peer lending services allow individuals to lend money to borrowers in exchange for interest payments. By participating in peer-to-peer lending opportunities, investors can receive passive income through interest payments on loans, which are normally paid out regularly.

Digital Items and Online Businesses: Creating and selling digital items, such as e-books, online courses, software, and digital downloads, can produce passive revenue for creators. Once digital products are made and marketed, they can be sold repeatedly to buyers, offering a source of passive revenue while producers sleep.

Affiliate Marketing: Affiliate marketing involves advertising items or services supplied by other companies and earning a commission on sales or referrals. By joining affiliate marketing schemes, individuals can earn passive income by promoting products through their website, blog, social media channels, or email list and receiving commissions on purchases produced through their referral links.

Automated Online Businesses: Building automated online businesses, such as e-commerce stores, drop-shipping enterprises, or membership sites, can produce passive revenue by employing automation technologies and systems to handle sales, customer care, and fulfillment operations. Once set up, automated web enterprises can earn cash around the clock with minimal ongoing effort.

In short, the concept of making money while sleeping involves building passive income streams that continue to generate cash even while individuals are not actively working. By investing in assets, generating intellectual property, utilizing digital platforms, and building automated systems, individuals can produce passive income and grow wealth over time, allowing them to achieve financial freedom and independence.

LIFE PARTNER AND BUSINESS COOPERATION

Life partners and business cooperation can play key roles in assisting wealth-making pursuits in numerous ways.

1. **Shared Goals and Values:** Life partners who share common financial goals and values can provide mutual support and encouragement in pursuing wealth-making possibilities. When both partners are aligned in their financial ambitions, they may work together to build plans, make financial decisions, and handle difficulties effectively.

2. **Pooling Resources:** Life partners can pool their resources, including income, savings, investments, and assets, to harness

their combined financial power and boost their wealth-making chances. By combining resources, partners can access greater investment possibilities, purchase properties, or create enterprises that may be beyond the grasp of individual efforts.

3. **Division of labor and knowledge:** In corporate cooperation, partners can exploit each other's strengths, talents, and knowledge to boost productivity and efficiency in wealth-making activities. By splitting duties, responsibilities, and roles based on individual talents and interests, partners can streamline operations, optimize performance, and achieve greater outcomes together.

4. **Emotional Support and Motivation:** Life partners and business partners can provide emotional support and motivation during tough times, setbacks, or periods of uncertainty. Having a supportive spouse can raise morale, provide reassurance, and help individuals stay focused and resilient in

pursuing their wealth-making goals.

5. **Risk Sharing and Mitigation:**
Partnership in wealth-making pursuits allows participants to share risks and limit potential losses. By distributing risk among numerous individuals or businesses, partners can limit exposure to financial setbacks, market changes, and unforeseen occurrences that may influence wealth-building efforts.

6. **complimentary talents and views:** Life partners and business partners typically bring complementary talents, views, and experiences to the table, enriching the decision-making process and boosting problem-solving capabilities. Partners with various experiences and expertise can bring fresh insights, inventive solutions, and alternate approaches to wealth-making difficulties.

7. **Networking and Connections:** Life partners and business partners can expand their networks and connections by using each other's relationships, contacts, and

professional networks. Networking opportunities created by partnerships can lead to new business prospects, strategic alliances, and significant industry connections that help wealth-making pursuits.

8. **Long-Term Planning and Legacy Building:** Life partners can engage in long-term financial planning and legacy building to assure the sustainability and continuity of wealth for future generations. By identifying agreed-upon goals, building thorough estate plans, and implementing wealth transfer methods, partners may create a lasting legacy and secure financial well-being for their families and loved ones.

In summary, life partners and business cooperation can support wealth-making endeavors by sharing goals and values, pooling resources, leveraging complementary skills and expertise, providing emotional support and motivation, sharing risks and mitigating losses, expanding networks and connections, and collaborating on long-term planning and legacy building. By working together synergistically, partners can optimize their potential for financial success, reach their wealth-making goals, and build a wealthy future together.

CHAPTER 4
CREATING A NEW ENVIRONMENT TO CREATE WEALTH

The environment has a crucial role in wealth-making by influencing economic possibilities, corporate circumstances, innovation, and individual success. Here are many ways in which the environment helps with wealth-making:

1. **"Economic Conditions"**: A friendly economic climate defined by stable economic growth, low inflation, low unemployment, and favorable monetary and fiscal policies gives prospects for wealth development. A strong economy provides a fertile foundation for entrepreneurship, investment, and employment, allowing individuals and corporations to produce money and accumulate wealth.

2. **Business environment:** A supportive

business environment containing infrastructure, institutions, rules, and access to money supports entrepreneurship, innovation, and business growth. Well-developed infrastructure, including transportation, communication, energy, and technology, enables firms to function efficiently and reach markets more effectively, contributing to wealth creation and economic development.

3. **Access to Markets and Customers:** Access to varied markets and customers is crucial for wealth-making prospects. A vibrant marketplace with powerful consumer demand, purchasing power, and market rivalry gives entrepreneurs and enterprises the possibility to innovate, develop products and services, and win market share, leading to income production and wealth accumulation.

4. **Technological breakthroughs:** Technological breakthroughs and innovation fuel wealth creation by enabling businesses

to boost productivity, cut costs, and create products and services. Access to technology, digital infrastructure, and research and development capabilities stimulates innovation and entrepreneurship, generating new chances for wealth production across businesses and sectors.

5. **Education and Human Capital:** A well-educated and talented workforce is crucial for wealth generation and economic prosperity. Investments in education, training, and human capital development enhance workforce productivity, creativity, and innovation, empowering individuals to pursue higher-paying jobs, entrepreneurial ventures, and career advancement opportunities that contribute to wealth accumulation and economic growth.

6. **Political Stability and Rule of Law:** Political stability, good governance, and the rule of law create an enabling environment for wealth-making by fostering investor confidence, preserving property rights, and

providing legal and regulatory clarity. Transparent and accountable governance structures, effective legal frameworks, and respect for the rule of law facilitate business transactions, contractual agreements, and investment activities, supporting economic development and wealth creation.

7. **Access to Financial Services:** Access to financial services, including banking, credit, insurance, and investment options, is vital for wealth-building programs. Financial inclusion projects that provide access to financial services to underprivileged groups, promote savings, allow access to credit, and encourage investment in productive assets can empower individuals and communities to acquire assets, generate income, and achieve financial security.

8. **Social Capital and Networks:** Social capital, including social networks, relationships, and community connections, can enhance wealth-making opportunities by offering access to knowledge, resources, and

support networks. Strong social links, teamwork, and community participation enable entrepreneurship, knowledge sharing, and collaborative action, empowering individuals and communities to seek economic possibilities and create shared prosperity.

In summary, the environment significantly contributes to wealth-making by shaping economic conditions, fostering entrepreneurship and innovation, facilitating access to markets and customers, driving technological advancements, investing in education and human capital, promoting political stability and the rule of law, expanding access to financial services, and leveraging social capital and networks. By establishing an enabling environment that supports economic growth, innovation, and individual success, societies may drive wealth creation, raise living standards, and promote inclusive and sustainable development for all.

The Spiritual Environment Supports Wealth Generation.

Spiritual encounters, frequently connected with personal growth, fulfillment, and inner transformation, can indirectly contribute to wealth generation through numerous mechanisms:

1. **Clarity of Purpose:** Spiritual encounters can offer individuals clarity of purpose, enabling them to recognize their passions, talents, and values. By connecting their behaviors and endeavors with their spiritual beliefs and values, individuals may pursue professional pathways, company ventures, or investment possibilities that resonate with their real selves, leading to greater fulfillment and success in their wealth-making pursuits.

2. **Mindset and Attitude:** Spiritual

encounters can build a favorable mindset and attitude toward prosperity and plenty. By nurturing concepts of prosperity, appreciation, and giving, individuals may adopt a more spacious attitude that draws riches and opportunity into their lives. A positive attitude toward wealth-making can drive individuals to take daring actions, overcome hurdles, and seize possibilities for financial growth and happiness.

3. **Creativity and invention:** Spiritual encounters can stimulate creativity, intuition, and invention, uncovering fresh views and ideas for wealth development. By tapping into their inner wisdom and intuition, individuals may discover unique ideas, company concepts, or investment strategies that have the potential to generate money and create value for themselves and others.

4. **Resilience and Adaptability:** Spiritual encounters can foster resilience, adaptability, and emotional intelligence,

enabling individuals to handle challenges, setbacks, and uncertainties in their wealth-making journey. By developing inner strength and resilience, individuals can overcome challenges, learn from failures, and persevere in the pursuit of their financial goals, ultimately boosting their potential to generate money and achieve success.

5. **Alignment with Values and Ethics:** Spiritual encounters typically highlight values such as integrity, honesty, compassion, and ethical conduct. By aligning their wealth-making endeavors with their spiritual values and principles, individuals may prioritize ethical business practices, sustainable investment strategies, and social responsibility initiatives that contribute to the greater good while generating wealth in a meaningful and sustainable manner.

6. **Connection and Collaboration:** Spiritual encounters can generate a sense of connection, community, and collaboration

among like-minded persons who share common spiritual views and ideals. By joining supportive groups, networking events, or spiritual gatherings, individuals may establish meaningful relationships, exchange ideas, and collaborate on wealth-making efforts that benefit themselves and others.

7. **Intuition and Decision-Making:**
Spiritual encounters can strengthen intuition, intuition, and intuition-based decision-making skills, enabling individuals to make informed choices and negotiate complex financial decisions with better clarity and understanding. By trusting their intuition and inner direction, individuals may make smart investments, company decisions, or career shifts that correspond with their highest purpose and lead to long-term wealth creation and fulfillment.

In summary, while spiritual encounters may not directly generate wealth, they can act as catalysts for personal growth, mentality reform, and inner alignment that indirectly contribute to wealth generation. By fostering clarity of purpose, a positive mindset, creativity, resilience, ethical conduct, connection, and intuition, spiritual encounters can empower individuals to pursue wealth-making endeavors with authenticity, purpose, and integrity, ultimately leading to greater success and fulfillment in their financial journey.

CHAPTER 5
CONCLUSION

Building money is a multidimensional process that requires a combination of strategic financial planning, disciplined habits, and a proactive mentality. Here is a conclusion on how to generate money by incorporating information from numerous sources:

1. **Financial Literacy:** A core part of wealth-building is financial literacy. Educate yourself on basic financial ideas, investment methods, and personal money management. This knowledge creates the basis for informed decision-making.

2. **Budgeting and Saving:** Establish a budget that specifies your income, spending, and savings goals. Prioritize saving a percentage of your money regularly. Consistent saving, even in small amounts, is

vital for building a financial cushion and creating chances for investing.

3. **Investment Diversification:** Diversify your investments across different asset types, such as stocks, bonds, real estate, and other instruments. Diversification helps disperse risk and boosts the potential for profits. Consider your risk tolerance, investment goals, and time horizon when designing an investment strategy.

4. **Continuous Learning and Skill Development:** Invest in your skills and education continually. Improving your abilities makes you more competitive in the labor market, boosts your earning potential, and opens up prospects for career growth.

5. **Entrepreneurship and Business Ownership:** Consider entrepreneurship or owning a business as a source of wealth generation. Entrepreneurial ventures can provide avenues for unlimited income potential, but they also come with risks.

Thoroughly research and plan before starting a business.

6. **Passive Income Sources:** Explore and establish passive income sources. Investments that generate passive income, such as dividends, rental income, or royalties, contribute to wealth accumulation without constant active effort.

7. **Financial Discipline and Delayed Gratification:** Practice financial discipline and accept delayed gratification. Avoid unnecessary debt, live within your means, and make mindful spending decisions. Delaying current wants for long-term financial goals is a vital part of gaining wealth.

8. **Networking and Relationship Building:** Build a strong network and nurture relationships within your sector. Networking can lead to career opportunities, business partnerships, and valuable insights. Surround yourself with individuals who

share similar financial goals and principles.

9. **Mindset and Positive Energy:** Cultivate a positive mindset toward wealth-building. Believe in your ability to achieve financial success, be open to opportunities, and approach challenges with resilience. Positive energy can attract opportunities and contribute to your overall well-being.

10**. Adaptability to Market Trends:** Stay informed about market trends, economic conditions, and industry developments. Being adaptable to changes in the market allows you to identify new opportunities, make informed decisions, and adjust your wealth-building strategies accordingly.

11. **Social and Environmental Responsibility:** Integrate social and environmental responsibility into your wealth-building approach. Consider investments or business opportunities that align with sustainable and ethical practices, contributing to a positive social impact.

12**. Leadership Planning:** Plan for the long

term and consider how your wealth-building efforts can contribute to a lasting legacy. This may involve estate planning, philanthropy, or passing down financial knowledge to future generations.

In conclusion, building wealth is a holistic endeavor that involves a combination of financial knowledge, strategic planning, disciplined habits, continuous learning, and a positive mindset. By incorporating these principles into your financial journey, you can create a solid foundation for long-term wealth accumulation and financial well-being.

Wealth and Nation-Building

Wealth, when distributed and managed effectively, can improve the standard of living in a country in several ways:

1. Increased Access to Basic Needs:
Wealth enables governments and societies to

invest in infrastructure, healthcare, education, and social welfare programs, ensuring that citizens have access to essential services and resources. Improved access to clean water, sanitation, healthcare facilities, and quality education enhances the overall well-being and quality of life for individuals and communities.

2. **Higher Employment Opportunities:** Wealth creation stimulates economic growth and creates employment opportunities across various sectors of the economy. As businesses expand, invest in innovation, and pursue new ventures, they create jobs and income opportunities for workers, reducing unemployment rates and providing individuals with the means to support themselves and their families.

3. **Rising Incomes and Standards of Living:** Economic prosperity resulting from wealth creation leads to rising incomes and standards of living for individuals and households. Increased disposable income

allows people to afford better housing, nutrition, clothing, and consumer goods, improving their overall quality of life and satisfaction.

4. Investment in Infrastructure and Public Services: Wealth generated through taxation, public-private partnerships, and foreign investments can be channeled into developing and maintaining critical infrastructure, such as roads, bridges, public transportation, energy systems, and communication networks. Access to reliable infrastructure enhances mobility, connectivity, and productivity, laying the foundation for sustained economic growth and development.

5. **Healthcare and Social Services:** Wealth enables governments to invest in healthcare systems, social services, and safety nets that promote public health, social equity, and well-being. Accessible healthcare services, preventive care, disease control measures, and social assistance programs support

vulnerable populations, reduce health disparities, and improve overall health outcomes, contributing to a healthier and more resilient society.

6. **Education and Skill Development:** Investing in education and skill development initiatives helps individuals acquire the knowledge, skills, and capabilities needed to participate in the workforce, innovate, and contribute to economic growth. Accessible and quality education opportunities empower individuals to unlock their full potential, pursue meaningful careers, and improve their socioeconomic status, ultimately raising the overall human capital and productivity of the nation.

7. **Innovation and Technological Advancement:** Wealth creation fosters innovation, research, and technological advancement, driving productivity gains, efficiency improvements, and economic diversification. Investment in research and development, technology transfer, and

innovation ecosystems stimulates entrepreneurship, fosters creativity, and positions countries at the forefront of global competitiveness, leading to sustained economic growth and prosperity.

8. **Cultural and Recreational Opportunities:** Wealthier societies often have greater access to cultural, recreational, and leisure activities that enrich people's lives and promote social cohesion. Investments in arts, culture, sports, parks, and recreation facilities enhance the quality of life, foster community engagement, and contribute to a vibrant and inclusive society.

In summary, wealth can improve the standard of living in a country by facilitating access to basic needs, creating employment opportunities, raising incomes and standards of living, investing in infrastructure and public services, promoting healthcare and social services, supporting education and skill development, fostering innovation and technological advancement, and providing cultural and recreational opportunities. By harnessing wealth effectively and promoting inclusive growth, countries can enhance the well-being and prosperity of their citizens, fostering sustainable development and shared prosperity for generations to come.

www.ingramcontent.com/pod-product-compliance
Lightning Source LLC
Chambersburg PA
CBHW071101290526
45795CB00004B/1603